Pork Fluff

Sundress Publications • Knoxville, TN

Book Editor: Rita Mookerjee
Managing Editor: Krista Cox
Editorial Assistants: Kanika Lawton, Whitney Cooper
Editorial Interns: Mia Grace Davis, Nic Job, Scott Sorensen

Colophon: This book is set in Goudy Old Style.

Cover Art and Design: Kristen Ton

Book Design: Erin Elizabeth Smith

Pork Fluff
Tiffany Hsieh

Table of Contents

III

IV

V

For Ba & Ma

I

Exhibit A

Me, age nine, Taichung. I'm sitting at the dining table, slumped with both legs curled up on the chair in front of my chest, face visibly upset. Before me, a few loose greasy-looking bamboo leaves. Zongzi, or sticky rice dumplings. Behind me, the kitchen, visibly small and dark, lights off. On the counter, a beat-up pot and rice cooker, the kind that keeps the rice warm for hours. Right of it, a brown wooden cabinet full of Ba's pottery teapots, a glare on the glass. Left of it, a brown wooden pantry shelf, bottles of soy sauce and rice wine in the middle. Beside me, two chairs with tall, brown, ornamented wooden backs. Opposite me, out of frame, Ma wants me to finish the zongzi. I refuse. She forbids me from leaving the table because little children in Africa are starving and I'm spoiled. I cry. She says go on, I'll wait. I wail. She grabs the camera. She shoots.

Obasan's Pool

The water's always blue and I always slide in feet first. I always float on my back, float facedown. I'm ten, goggles new. I see palm trees around me and they are upside down, bent at the top. I flip on my side. I dive for the bottom. I pretend to be a shark. I circle around Obasan's fat ankles moon-walking in the shallow end. I blow bubbles like a fish. I make my way to the middle. I sit on the blue mosaics, legs crossed. I swim with my family at Obasan's and she has staff working to keep the water blue. I do my thing. I come up for air. I wonder if the staff can see a small yellow stream or green because of the blue. One of them looks very old.

Family History

They say Ah-gong died young, when I was two years old. They say he was a drunk who gambled his fortune away and left his debts to his family. Our family. They say he was ill-tempered and that his own children feared him. They say Ba, the only son, feared him the most. They say for sure he had held me in his arms, but the only photos I've seen of him are black and white with just him. They say he had a heart attack. They say he smoked cigars, too, and that's why. They say it's just as well that I don't remember a thing about him. They say remember this: Ah-gong was a doctor, and he was handsome. They say back then, that was something.

Arigatou, Sayonara

The Japanese came and left behind sashimi and sake in Ah-gong and Ah-ma's stomachs. They left behind ohayo gozaimasu in the morning and konnichiwa in the afternoon. I learned a Japanese nursery rhyme from Ah-gong and Ah-ma who learned it in school where the Japanese came and taught for fifty years. When they came, they came to be Ah-gong and Ah-ma's masters. When they left, they left behind moshi moshi on the telephone and tegami in the mail. Many years after they came and left, they also left behind NHK and sumo on Ah-gong and Ah-ma's television, tatami in their children's and grandchildren's new-build condos. I don't know why, but after a while, I half-stopped singing the Japanese nursery rhyme the same way Ah-gong and Ah-ma half-stopped bowing their heads, not quite arigatou, not quite sayonara.

Calculate Life

Ma says she went to see a Mr. Calculate Life, a very good one. He calculates people's lives based on the number of strokes in each of the characters in their names. Those numbers are then calculated with the date and time of their births in both ancient and modern Chinese calendars. Ma says this Mr. Calculate Life, a very detailed one, also calculated my numbers with the numbers he calculated for Ma and Ba. According to his final calculations, I'm likely to marry late and have a hard life. Ma says that means I'm unlikely to marry before my late twenties and unlikely to marry rich. It means I'm likely to go out working and come home cooking and cleaning. Ma says some people change their names to change the calculations in their life but that our Mr. Calculate Life, a very wise one, says I have a good name for a girl born on the same day as the emperor of Japan.

I Spy

I can eat six braised eggs in one day. They are prettier than strawberry ice cream. Sometimes I swallow watermelon seeds too and my friend says they'll grow trees in my belly. I secretly wish she's right. She lives with her ah-ma who makes her eat goji berries and sends her to Japan every summer. My ah-ma, the one who lives with us, has never been to Japan. She's always in her room listening to old Taiwanese songs on the radio when really I know she's spying on us. What's for dinner. Did Ma use the right soy sauce. How many eggs I ate. After school I hide under the piano in our living room and spy on her from behind the cover. Where she puts her teeth. Is she hiding snacks under the bed. Why her underwear is so big. Everybody says I'm lucky to have double eyelids like hers but they don't spy what I spy. She snores at night and farts during the day.

Tadpoles

I'm a super breaststroker, beating a freestyler by half a pool in Grade 5 and the whole school goes wild for me, especially the Grade 4s. They whisper my name when I walk down the hall. The Grade 3s are intimidated or shy, they gawk at me like I'm a hero. I go home feeling like I'm going to the Olympics and think about what country I'd swim for. What's Chinese Taipei? Who says they are from Japanese Tokyo or American Washington, D.C.? I imagine people cheering for me because I swim breaststroke faster than the freestylers. After, the interviewer wants to know what I want to say to people back home. I say it's my best stroke. It's the only stroke I learned when Ma signed me up for group lessons. They assembled us in the water like tadpoles and told us to kick.

Middle C

I play with Middle C a little too long and the other notes are mad at me. Teacher shows me how to play the notes together. She gives me a sticker every time I play them well. The notes are up and down Middle C in front of my belly button. Sometimes I play too many notes and my arms get sore. I play many notes every day for many days. One day I say the H word. Ma hands me a stick and says if you hate it so much, go ahead. I look around me and see so many stickers, so many notes. I look for Middle C but it's not there. It's not in the middle in front of my belly button. I take the stick. It's wood, three feet, two knots, and I was the one who found it up in the mountains, on the side of the road, in the middle of nowhere.

Scarred

This here on my chin is from when I accidentally branded myself with incense trying to steal candy during bai-bai. Ah-ma had said her prayers to Ah-gong and the gods, and I reached for the candy without seeing the burning stick staked there while the dead ate. Down here, on my right foot, that's from a scooter's exhaust pipe. It was a family outing to the rice paddies, and I was wearing slippers. Up here, on the left, I was hit by a swing. The doctor gave me nine stitches and a big white bandage around the head. For a while they thought I was going to be less bright. And here, my two front teeth, they are fake. I was playing Shark Attack on a marble slide with my brother. He was the shark. His wife didn't come home with him last Christmas, and I asked about it at dinner. It's none of your business, he snapped. No hesitation, no eye contact.

Fake Teeth

We didn't play Shark Attack anymore after I face-planted on a marble slide and banged my two front teeth. He pushed, she fell, me and my brother each told as I bared the cleaved teeth to Ma's horror. I had been in a storytelling competition before that. The story was about two sheep and a goat. What I wanted to show and tell about my two fake front teeth was that they were like those knee-high socks that made your legs look like a geisha's face. Underneath it, one tooth had its nerves severed, pulled out, and replaced with a pin. The other had a live nerve intact and Big Uncle, the dentist who got me the fake teeth, said it would die on its own, but it didn't. Hasn't. For years, Big Uncle made me a new set of fake choppers every now and then and glued them on with his super dental glue. There, he'd say, all pretty again.

Moon and Back

My brother would deny this now, but a long time ago he told me about a number you could dial, hang up, and the phone would ring back. Ma picked up and said Wei? Wei? She fell for it every single time. One time a lady operator came on the other end and said stop playing with the phone or else. It didn't ring back after that. I tried random numbers. One was the shortest to dial on the finger wheel. Zero was the longest. We watched an American movie. After that, I dialed a lot of zeros in case E.T. got home. I liked to turn the finger wheel all the way to the right and watch it turn back to the left on its own. Like to the moon and back. My brother said he was going to be like Neil Armstrong. Back then we knew Armstrong as 阿姆斯特朗, and my brother, he was going to be the first Chinese person to walk on the moon.

II

—

Church on Queen

Our people ran a church on Queen. We didn't know what kind of people we should be gathering with in the beginning or where we should be gathering with them. We went to the church on Queen on Sundays when our people gathered. We gathered with them to have potlucks, buy a used car, play softball, sing. Some of our people prayed and we prayed with them. We bowed our heads peeping. We opened the Bible pretending. We listened to the sermon slouching. We made friends with some of our people who we sometimes gathered with on days other than Sundays and in places other than the church on Queen. Most of them we wouldn't have been friends with back home but here they are our people and we are friends.

About a Fish

The fish flipped like crazy on the floor of a supermarket. He must have escaped the tank or slipped out of the net used to scoop him out. He was a dark silver and flipped like crazy. A man standing next to the tank went after the fish with a broomstick. The fish's eyes bulged in opposite directions as the broomstick came down on him. Whack. And again. Whack, whack. I saw a metallic grey that flipped like crazy. A fly landed on a nearby shelf. A man walking past had a dead fish double-bagged in see-through plastic. A family was going to have fish head soup with sliced ginger and green onions. For two months I saw the fish eye from my childhood. It was white and opaque and floated in clear broth like a bobber.

Balloon, Typhoons, Afternoon

At least six times I've had this exact dream: I'm an egg-shaped balloon swimming in the clouds with little short fat limbs that don't move; a typhoon comes four or five times and four out of five times somebody is cooking something with Shaoxing rice wine; there are two or three songs I know all the words to, one is in Japanese and doesn't count; in Grade 1 I gave half a pair of my shoes to somebody in the class; in Grade 3 I thought you had to read a thousand thousand-year-old books to be like Indiana Jones; I don't actually believe in colons or semi-colons; after supper there are roughly ninety million popcorns in the ceiling; I have one request in most cases; a fly circling the lamp beside my bed is found dead on the carpet in the afternoon.

Bullying

You summoned me to your office over the intercom. You said what you working on, I said I'm working on an article about bullying. You said what's that again, I said bullying. You made a face that said huh and I knew I said something wrong. You were the boss. I was ESL. I wanted to die in your office and bury myself in my ESL sleeves. I said you know, bullies. You had this look on your face and said *bul-ly-ing*. Those thin mustache-free lips of yours moved like jellyfish in slo-mo and I saw *bul-ly-ing* pronounced in three syllables, not *bul-lying* in two syllables the way I was saying. Deep down I was grateful to have this mispronunciation corrected, but my mouth was too fish-on-a-hook to say thanks. My cover was blown. I was ESL, not from here, not supposed to write. I could tell my missed pronunciation had angered you and your must-ache lips. They convulsed when you fixed your gaze on me and said you have to pronounce the *y*, said *bul-ly-ing*, said *ing*, said say it. I swallowed and said *bully-in*, said *bull-y-in*, said *bully-yin-g*.

Girl and Her Hair

Girl had naturally wavy hair, or so she said it was natural. She said even though she permed her hair in grades four, five, six, her ah-ma's ah-ma's ancestors had Portuguese blood from ancient times and her ba had a kink or two in his hair too. Girl said, Screw the *student head*, the hairstyle required for all girls in grades seven, eight, nine, ten, eleven, twelve. Straight, ear-length, no bangs, no layers, no dyes, no perms, no products, the uniform-like *student head* was the closest thing that resembled communism in Taiwan. You got the ruler on your palms if you went a quarter-inch too long or you looked like you did something to your hair other than combing it. Every time Girl got the ruler, her hands stung and she couldn't practise the double bass, an instrument she picked for not wanting to pick the piano or the violin like everyone else did. She had just finished grade eight when her family said they were moving overseas to where she could have any hairstyle she liked. Purple, asymmetrical, moused, funky. Girl was naturally psyched, or so she said she was psyched. She said she would grow her hair long in grades nine, ten, eleven, twelve, thirteen. She said she would grow it until it got too much or too wavy, usually around the shoulders, then she would cut it and go back to the short hair she had, or had always liked, in grades one, two, three.

Two Big Macs

I had to explain to a white kid born here the difference between "there" and "their." His perfect English presented our project on *The Catcher in the Rye*, which I pretty much only sort of read as it's near impossible to catch all the rye bits when you've never played catch before. The teacher said, "Matt, that was really good!" Matt's not my English name. Mine was picked—I picked it from a list of girl names—the week before I started school here. Most of the time I prayed for my real name not to be called. The substitute managed to most of the time when taking attendance. I got some participation marks for paying attention and smiling. In our musical production of *Peter Pan*, I wanted to be like this girl Tracy, who played Peter, but I watched Wendy because she was so pretty and got to say "shit" in front of everyone. Ba and Ma said afterward they felt pressured from the other parents to stand and clap for as long as they did even though they saw me for three seconds total. Later, when Ah-gong and Ah-ma visited, Ba and Ma took them to see me in another role that was more front and center. I had a good voice. At my part-time job I got to call out to the kitchen, "Two Big Macs!"

Cafeteria

I went there once and stood watching a girl pass a fry to a guy mouth to mouth. She had smoky eyes and hoop earrings. He had a cap on backwards and studs in both ears. I wondered what it'd be like to be a girl like that, pass a fry like that, to a guy like that, sit in the cafeteria, eat and laugh, like that. I imagined the fry was salted and dipped in ketchup. I could taste the trans-fat in my mouth, the potato's mushy middle filling the gaps between my teeth. It was a limp fry, not perky. Its ends squared off like the bento Ba packed for me in my knapsack. But it was a french fry and it was born and raised to stand tall, like the Statue of Liberty, on a pedestal, in a cafeteria. They held school dances there, too, every now and then. I almost went to one and pictured lights dimming in my head. I almost went there and stood watching others getting fruit punch, doing the moonwalk, moving their body like in the movies. In the end, I knew I was doing myself a favor by waiting until I could dance like that, close my eyes and tap my feet, step to the left, step to the right, smile, turn, like that.

Boys from McDonald's

I liked a boy from McDonald's in high school. We both worked there, he on the grill, me on cash. We went to the woods behind the observatory once. He drove his parents' Mustang and brought a blanket and a bag of Lay's. We ate the Lay's and laid down on the blanket, which was more like a throw from his mother's couch. I thought that was sweet of him, to think of bringing a throw from his mother's couch. He laid on top of me and started kissing me. It was the second time we kissed and there was a lot more saliva than the first time, which was at another McDonald's boy's parents' basement. I thought the saliva must be how Caucasian boys kissed but it was hard to say because, at the time, he was the only boy I had ever kissed. I thought maybe there was more saliva the second time because we were in the woods with no one around us. After a while, he looked at me like he might want to take off my jeans. I looked at him, too, like maybe he might want to take off my jeans. I thought, if he wanted to take off my jeans, I'd probably let him. I also thought, if something bad were to happen to me, with him, my parents would be very sad about making the mistake of coming to Canada. But he didn't take off my jeans and I figured it was because the other McDonald's boy, who also worked on the grill and who was from Hong Kong, had said that time in his parents' basement that he'd kill him if he did something to me. I figured he'd said that because we were both Chinese, the other McDonald's boy and I, and he'd felt responsible for me as a fellow Chinese person. Something like that. His girlfriend was from Macao and I saw them kissing that time in the basement while the Caucasian boy was kissing me. I saw him, the other McDonald's boy, looking at me kissing while looking at him kissing.

Hot Stuff

This Korean boyfriend I had took me to McDonald's and asked would you mind paying for yourself. He was poor trying to be an artist and I kind of thought this would be a good story to tell our kids when he's famous someday and calls me sweetie at a cocktail party. We went back to his room where he put one condom over the other and made me take a Gravol afterwards in case one of the condoms broke. His housemates were philosophy majors who mocked each other all night long about Nietzsche, Kant, and Kierkegaard. I felt unintelligent around them. I wanted my Korean boyfriend, who was born here and knew who Nietzsche, Kant, and Kierkegaard were, to know how much I loved kimchi and pork bone soup. He didn't tell his friends I was a good pianist. He told them I was Chinese, to which someone cited Tao Te Ching. I smiled because they thought it was funny. I thought it was funny because my Korean boyfriend thought it was funny. I didn't think it was that funny when he broke up with me and said we didn't have much to talk about. I went to the bookstore and bought a book by Plato. I never read the whole thing or half of it but I became a journalist anyway after I stopped playing the piano. I interviewed my Korean ex-boyfriend on the phone about some hot stuff he was working on. He didn't recognize my name or voice and it was just as well. He didn't have anything to say that was of public interest so I ended the interview after ten minutes.

Legs and Pits

I shouldn't be the one to tell you this but girls here shave their legs and pits. That's all I'm gonna say about that. If you wanna know about how girls here get those nice calves with toned muscles, I can show you some stair exercises. There's also a certain type of running shoe they wear to make their calves look like that. No, not Nike. They don't look as good on women and they're more expensive. I got my Air Jordans last year for like a hundred bucks. Don't go telling Ba and Ma now. They don't need to know everything. They call that need-to-know here. You'll pick up these things. Plus, I wear my Air Jordans a lot. There are guys here who have a pair of shoes for walking, another pair for jogging, and several pairs for playing sports, one for each sport they play. Speaking of which, my buddy's coming over to shoot some hoops. Yeah, the Jewish one. I met him in math on my first day here and we sort of became friends. I joke that he's my Jewish brother. The two cultures are very similar. Both Chinese and Jewish people are smart and cheap! No, he's not born there. He's born here. His parents were born here. I've had meals in their house. I went to the synagogue with them once. I call his grandmother Bubba. No, he doesn't have a girlfriend. He has a sister. She's younger, too, maybe a year younger than you. She's on the swim team. I shouldn't be the one to tell you this but girls here use tampons.

In a Gutless Room

My doggy gets scared of the thunderstorm and I get scared for my doggy. The windows are thin and we start licking hemp oil together in our gutless air-conditioned room. But my doggy, scared shitless, she gets more scared and shitless as the thunder gets angrier and louder. I get us covered up in bed under the blanket. She gets huffing and puffing with her wet goon-like tongue. I get paranoid and paralyzed by doggy psychosis and what that's gonna do to my doggy. I try getting her to stop shaking. When she doesn't, I get worried and say, Come, let mommy see. It gets jumbled and comes out in Mandarin the way Ma would say it whenever I got scared as a kid. 來, 媽看. I don't know how this happens since I got no Mandarin for my doggy who's from Mississauga and she got no 媽 who's a doggy from Taiwan or China. But she seems to get it anyway, my doggy, that I got her under the blanket where we are waiting for the thunderstorm to get lost.

The Squirrel

Some dick has run over the squirrel's friend, the friend's tail sticking out like a hairpiece, the squirrel running in circles around his friend, my friend and I watching this unfold, watching the squirrel's cheeks deflate, his black eyes darting from fir to friend, friend to fir, their mouths open closed, open closed, the squirrel turning to face me, my wheels rolling in neutral, the squirrel's face reminding me of when my brother and I got separated from Ah-ma at the train station, Ah-ma's face on the platform, her feet running after the train, our feet touching the train, her hands reaching, her mouth open closed, open closed.

Still Life

She wakes up from her nap in the afternoon and wonders if anything in the house has changed, if, for example, the furnace has died. She looks at the things in the house and is convinced that some of the things she cleans up on a weekly basis, for example, sesame seeds from bagels, beard trimmings, cat hair, and dust, should be left alone to add depth. She hears in her head the Für Elise garbage truck music she grew up hearing in Taichung, and for a second or two, the house she's in is not surrounded by Ontario snow and it's not still January.

Bok Choy Love

Our anniversary comes like a squall during my drive home, a sixty-minute petrol-numbing waste of time. There I'm sitting in time and time's a petrified vegetation of slush. The black pickup in the rearview flashes its blinding headlights twice. Is the idiot signalling for me to move up two feet of vegetated time in a lowland of wheels and rims? Does the idiot not know that I'm using this time to think about our anniversary and the vegetables that would define our love? Must we, too, face the candlelight and order something that spirals up in the middle of a plate that's mostly rim and then be judged by the waiter who wants to know if we'll be having dessert? In slush, I idle like a lump of bok choy and wait for the lights to change.

Call Come Call Go

She calls him Ba the same way she called her ba Ba. She never calls him by name or Lao-gong or Honey or Dear. It has always been this way even though he's only four years older than her. She has always called him Ba, come or go, starting when she was teaching their children to call him Ba. But he does not call her Ma or Lao-po or Babe or Sweetheart or her name. If he needs to call her, come or go, she responds to the sound of his voice or throat clearing. If she doesn't hear him or is tending to the gardens outside the house, then he calls, come or go, in a louder voice, Ha-lo or Hello or Hey. They call come call go on fifteen acres of land on a country road where, at night, a distant neighboring dog can be heard whimpering softly to the moon.

III

In Hindsight

We didn't come here to be us. We came here to be like you. Ma and Ba paid money to come and my brother and I left our homework undone. There was no upheaval or war. And just like that we were here like you but it was unclear if we were anything alike. We didn't tan like you. We didn't entertain like you. We didn't tango-skate like you in those tango outfits like yours. Here we came to be. There we worshipped your alphabets and movie stars and french fries. We longed to be like you while we were most likely just being ourselves. And just like that we liked you and we liked to think you liked us, too. After all, Ma and Ba paid a price to come and my brother and I played our parts to stay.

Half Night

The house has a long driveway with a single detached garage and a walkway next to it and to the side door that takes you straight to the heart where the kitchen's to the back and the living room's to the front and all in all the wife says the feng shui's okay in terms of facings to the sun and the stop signs and the traffic flow that goes right by the house instead of coming head-on to a T which can only lead to a car flying through the front window one of these days and to the husband heading to his death while contemplating by the window what the people next door are going to do about the maple leaves that the wind blows to their half of the property and if another wind will blow them back to the people next door since no one knows which half of the wind will blow during half night when half of their kids are asleep and the other half a sleep away from being blown across the ocean back to where they came from.

Feelings

My piano teacher says I'm not playing with enough emotions. She's from Hong Kong and likes to say more feelings here and more feelings there. She likes to say this while tapping the eraser end of her pencil on the score. Sometimes she writes more feelings right over the bars where she wants me to play with more emotions. She says Chopin's one of the most romantic composers and I need to have more feelings here and here and here and all the way there. She asks me to play again. This time she's standing behind me, pushing my upper body and trying to stir up some feelings. She tells Ma my homework's to watch *Gone With the Wind* so I can feel deep emotions and passion. She blushes when she says this. Her hair's cropped and permed. I can't picture her having sex with her husband.

Persimmons

I suppose it's not nice of me to dismiss a plate of sliced persimmon Ma pushes in front of me and she goes on about how this is the fruit Ah-gong used to bring home when he came back from being away on a business trip and that the persimmons from Japan are the best meaning they are more delicious and exquisite and expensive and rare because they are from Japan or at least imported from Japan and this is the fruit Ah-gong always brought home from his business trips and this is what Ma remembers when she sees persimmons in her local supermarket long after Ah-gong's gone and feels the need to buy them and bring them home to wash and cut up in the kitchen sink and offer them to me the same way they were offered to her because this is the fruit she ate when she was a child after waiting for Ah-gong to come home even though it's hardly a fruit she enjoys and you can tell as she bites a small corner off the persimmon with her denture and says it's sweet like she was not expecting it like it's the first time she's tasted a persimmon.

The Common Trap

It rained the other day and I thought about how I used to say I like the rain. I used to say things that were the opposite of what others said. I did that not because I felt like opposing others but because I felt sorry for the things others dismissed as not as good or basically bad. I used to think it was just me and I was the only one who felt sorry for things like the end piece of a loaf of bread or a restaurant with no customers. And then that movie *The Joy Luck Club* came out and every Chinese girl and their mothers who went to see it cried their eyes out over the "bad crab...best quality heart" scene. I knew then that feeling sorry for bad things was a common trap. Because if you didn't eat the bad crab, who would? Would the bad crab feel bad if no one ate it, or would Ma, who cooked the bad crab, feel bad if no one ate it? Was the crab bad or was the cooking of that crab bad? Was the fact that you ate the bad crab bad or the fact that you were bad and that's why you ate the bad crab? What was more bad, eating the bad crab and having the best quality heart or eating the best crab and having the worst quality heart? These are just some of questions you ask yourself when getting that bad crab feeling.

Rabbit Hole

The upstairs carpet has not been cleaned for two weeks and the squirrel knows this. He climbs up the Virginia creeper and squats and looks. By now the dog's used to a rodent showing up like this but I'm not. She's the talented one, the dog. A few days ago she did a Jackson Pollock on the carpet. It took her three days to get the hang of it. The last splash was a dash of yellow and white that dotted between the Poäng and a piece of freeze-dried beef liver. I administer milk thistle for the dog's liver and goat's milk for her bleat of a river. It's sizzling out and you can feel the heat by looking at the weather app. Out the window, down below, a rabbit appears in the yard. Hubby thinks it's a she. She's digging and making room for more rabbits. Did I tell you I was a forty-one-year-old rabbit the year Ah-gong died? It was an inauspicious year for rabbits to be facing death and Ma put some special grass in my shirt pocket to ward off evil at the funeral. We burned the grass back at the hotel and watched it shrivel into flaky black bits against the bathroom white of the sink. I remember thinking we were going to set off the fire alarm.

Lemons

He waves his hand in a fish and chips place the way Chinese people holler at servers in Chinese restaurants. He asks for lemons by saying lemons but his wife says can we have some lemons please. He ignores this, her trying to tell him what to say in English or how to say it as if he didn't know how to ask for what he wanted. A thin slice of lemon floats in his glass of water and he takes the straw and stabs it pulpless while waiting. He makes little noises with his mouth and flags down a waitress holding a coffee pot. She has a smile at least and he says this time can I have some lemons. The waitress says yes I'll be right back but she's still pouring coffee at the adjacent table and the one after that and chatting. He drums his fingers now too close to the fork and knife until someone brings him two teeny lemon wedges. He says okay okay but his wife says thank you. He grunts at this, at her trying to imply that he doesn't know how to say thank you in English or that he should say thank you for two teeny lemon wedges. He considers not tipping the way Chinese people consider not tipping in Chinese restaurants. But he's hungry and his nose's running over the batter-thick halibut.

Steal Eat

She heats up a bowl of rice drizzled with pork fat. She adds a splash of soy sauce to the steaming heap and squats down on a foot stool in the kitchen to steal eat. Hidden from her first daughter, who tells her pork fat is bad for her high cholesterol and high blood pressure, and her second daughter, who tells her the only people who still eat pork fat in Taiwan are the poor people, she devours the fat, soy sauce, and rice with a pair of wooden chopsticks dulling at the tip. She recalls how, after the occupation ended and the Japanese had gone home and she got married, she saved drops of pork fat after her in-laws had finished the pork she cooked. She recalls how, while everyone else napped in the afternoon and she had finished washing and cleaning the pigs in the pigsty, she stole ate a bowl of rice drizzled with pork fat and stole read a book in Japanese.

Kill Price

Saturday morning and she goes shopping at the Taichung Fifth Market. She picks up two fish heads for the price of one from the fish lady whose daughter sells slippers and fly swatters in the adjacent stand. She passes by the bean lady next and picks up a bag of pears from the fruit lady across the aisle who always throws in one or two more for free. Outside, she checks out the imported T-shirts, hoodies, and jeans from the U.S. and proceeds to kill price with the merchant before opening her purse. After that, she swings by the breakfast stall and orders four sets of egg pancakes, baked bread, deep-fried dough sticks, and soybean milk for less than what the fish lady's daughter was trying to sell her six plush Hello Kitty slippers from Hong Kong. By the time she's home, she's convinced she should have killed half-price off the T-shirts and makes a mental note to kill better next Saturday.

Lipstick

I almost stole a lipstick once. Back then, fourteen and not yet a citizen, I wanted to have without having to purchase a thing like a lipstick, which said I was vain and stupid. San-bah. If I had purchased a thing like that, there'd be a transaction, a receipt. There'd be proof that I wanted to be pretty, which I thought was pretty lame. I took the lipstick at Shoppers Drug Mart and held it in my hand. I thought about putting it back on the rack, I put it back, then I took it in my hand again. I must have done that one too many times because the store clerk cornered me and asked to see the contents of my bag. I hadn't decided to bag the lipstick but my hand was momentarily in my bag and the lipstick was in my hand. I tried explaining with my not-yet-fluent English that I was checking how much money I had. In truth, I knew I had none. I must have sounded overly defensive because I was asked to leave and I did so at once. Red-faced, what bothered me as I was leaving was not how I was caught almost stealing. It was the fact that I knew the store clerk was going to tell people about catching a Chinese girl almost stealing even though I could have been Japanese or Korean. Even though I'm not.

Pork Fluff

In the fifth-floor apartment of a building with no elevator, he was old and alone now because his wife had died first. One of his children lived nearby and arranged to have bento delivered to his door four times a week. Three times a week they had him over. Used to be three times bento and four times over when there were two of them. He didn't mind the new arrangement. He'd rather not eat at someone else's table, especially his daughter-in-law's. He never did like her cooking and his wife berated him every time he asked for pork fluff to go with his rice. She said if someone was going to have them over and feed them, especially their daughter-in-law, he should just be thankful and eat what was on the table. Now that he was old and alone because his wife had died first, he ate boiled broccoli for breakfast, doctor's orders. With each floret he added pork fluff right out of the bag. Sometimes fish fluff. He figured he would eat a whole plate of boiled broccoli if it meant he didn't have to sit on the toilet for a long time and be sore. He figured that was important in case there were more years left than necessary.

Baby Cuz

I like it better when Baby Cuz's ba calls my ma to say business's bad or business's so-so. But then he has to go and drop dead early in the hospital and yesterday Baby Cuz calls my ma, her gugu, to say how beautiful her ba was. She calls her gugu mornings to say she's thinking of moving to New York or Abu Dhabi. Ma calls me evenings to say did I tell you Baby Cuz's moving to New York or Abu Dhabi. Maybe it's better this way—Ma doesn't call Baby Cuz, who doesn't call her ma, who sometimes calls Ma, who always calls me if I don't call her—and I'm having a late reaction. I call Ma to say where's Baby Cuz moving to, New York or Abu Dhabi. Then we show up in the same crematorium in our home town, Baby Cuz and I. It's thirty-five degrees Celsius. We laugh a lot about a lot of nothing and bond like cuzes do over sticky dead cells and foods we don't digest anymore. We share a taxi to the same airport, separate gates, neither boarding for New York nor Abu Dhabi. Best conversation of our lives and I mean it.

Pinky Swear

For the record, I didn't show up at the Taichung Train Station. I'm sure the two of you didn't, either. I'm sure when the three of us pinky-swore we'd meet in front of the Taichung Train Station in twenty years, it was just us being silly together, like when we swore we'd marry a boy band and be wives together. We never said twenty years from which date or at what time. For the record, I've always thought it'd be in the morning, around eight or nine. I've always pictured one of us standing there wearing an old lady's dress and holding an old lady's purse and waiting like an old lady with time to spare. I've always wondered if whoever showed up first would be standing in front of the train station and waiting all day or what. And then when it was roughly twenty years later, I didn't feel old enough to be standing in front of the train station wearing an old lady's dress and holding an old lady's purse and waiting like an old lady. I know I sound like an asshole but at the time I didn't think it was practical to get on a transpacific flight just to show up at the Taichung Train Station over a twenty-year-old pinky swear. For the record, I thought about it and the thought of that makes me think about how I thought about going back to Taichung to the train station wearing an old lady's dress and holding an old lady's purse and waiting.

IV

Black Limousine

I don't remember your name but I remember you. Those summers we spent swimming at your ah-ma's but you'd rather play inside, in your room which had its own living room. You showed me a framed picture of your ma and said she'd come for you one day. Even then I knew you knew she wouldn't but you said it as if it were true. Besides, you said, you could go live with your ba and your new half-brother. But that, too, I knew you knew you wouldn't stay longer than a few days and you wouldn't have a room with its own living room. But you said it as if it were true and I played along waiting for someone to walk in any moment and take you away in a black limousine. After they said you ran away, I looked into every tinted window of every black limousine on the Sanmins, Taipings, Wuchuans. I still do, on the Bloors, Eglintons, Lake Shores, in case you are in the backseat, in case it's true.

The Fat Nun

She'd have to be ancient now. We used to wait for her rounded figure to cross the courtyard. Like a penguin marching. The fat nun. She was the only nun in our school who rode a bright red Vespa and whistled with two fingers. We waited for a glimpse of her by the second-floor railing where a row of betel palms provided good camouflage. We thought nuns didn't get periods. But if a nun were to get her period and have a blood stain on the back of her skirt, we knew it'd be the fat nun. She taught the seniors math and laughed like an opera singer. The happiest nun we ever saw. We wondered whether she really loved being a nun or she just loved not having her period. We were convinced the older nuns gave their meals away to be like Mother Teresa. We prayed for the fat nun to not be like them. One of us knew how to make a cross. Two of us put our palms together the way our parents did in front of incense. We told ourselves God wouldn't mind.

Sleep Stuffed

A friend of mine has invited me over to talk about whether she should stay in North America or go back to Taiwan for good. The house she lives in is the house her family back home paid for with stock money. She's the only one here unless she's seeing someone but even then, she doesn't like having them around after doing it. She tells me this in Mandarin while serving me instant coffee. You're so lucky, she says, you look like you're sleep stuffed with no puffy eyes. My friend is not the nerdy type but she's the only one I know who has two master's degrees, one of them an MBA. She'd get a DMA, too, a Doctor of Musical Arts, if her family wasn't still in debt from the last market crash. Her grand plan is to marry a doctor or lawyer. They wouldn't be home most of the time and she'd be able to read books and play the piano all day long. I'm not like you, she switches to English and says, I need to feel loved and I feel more loved when I have family close by and someone calls me to dinner. When I feel loved, she switches back to Mandarin, I sleep more stuffed. I gulp down the instant coffee and tell her to stay with me anyway.

Two Years Later

He came as a visa student two years before his ba ma did. So that two years later, when his ba ma joined him, he thought they looked fresh off the boat and they thought he looked like a foreign kid. He was both excited and embarrassed to be seen in public with his ba ma but took them to a large supermarket chain anyway. He explained Cheerios to them and showed them how milk bags worked with a milk bag pitcher he then put in the shopping cart along with things like ketchup, frozen fruit punch, and McCain fries. In the bulk section, he scooped up a bag of jelly beans and ate one to demonstrate how the bulk section worked. He ate a few more jelly beans as he took his ba ma from aisle to aisle, picking up things like Windex, paper towels, and Ziploc bags. He was explaining a tuna sandwich to them in the canned food section when a security guard approached him and accused him of eating the jelly beans without first paying for them by weight. He was offended and felt that this would not have happened had the security guard not been an immigrant or had his ba ma not looked so fresh off the boat. His ba ma, on the other hand, felt very lose face and that this would not have happened had their son not looked or acted like a foreign kid. And because he was sixteen, the security guard banned him, not his ba ma, from entering the supermarket chain for two years. So that two years later, when a Chinese supermarket opened in town and his ba ma took him there, he thought they looked foreign among other Chinese shoppers and they thought he looked like a Chinese kid in a candy store, homesick for things like shrimp snacks, instant noodles, and plum lollipops.

Titanic

My piano student came here on a boat when she was two years old. Maybe that's why she wants to learn how to play that song from *Titanic*. She was there and a part of her goes on and on. Week after week, my piano student talks to me about boys. She places her hands on the keys as she talks, her nails long and polished, her fingers flat like water. She wants me to play for her instead. I don't know why I give into her purple-shadowed puppy eyes. Bit by bit, I let my piano student talk me into helping her quit piano. We go rollerblading by her house, her idea of Big Sisters. Her mother shows me how to make Vietnamese spring rolls. Her father asks where I'm from and smiles with half of his mouth that I have no sea in me like his daughter does. That I'm more grounded somehow. We have our picture taken on the front steps. We are both in shorts and short sleeves. My piano student looks older than sixteen. Her makeup is all wrong, her posture too ladylike. I tell her she doesn't need all that stuff on her face, but she hands me a Sprite and tells me about getting a job at the music store, about the guy at the music store, goes on about his motorcycle and leather jacket, goes on and on.

Million Bucks

The Vietnamese lady on Queen East gave me a haircut for $8. In 1999, the end was coming and you couldn't get a chocolate bar with fat almonds for $8. I looked up for things to fall out of the sky: a goose, a rock, a spaceship. I could get a junior stylist haircut but you'd have to be Type A not to try an $8 one, tell your ma about it, and watch her squint with pride and envy and, later, profound distress. Why so cheap? Why you not pay more for better hair? How she make money? How you not scared? Then somebody said I looked like Cameron Diaz in *There's Something About Mary*. A complete stranger looked at my $8 hair and saw a Chinese Cameron. That's worth a million bucks. I went out for a walk. A bird dropped shit on my head. It was a seagull and I never saw it coming.

Cooking Videos

I watch cooking videos on YouTube every night. I watch them in bed under the blanket wearing nothing but a tank top and underwear. The cooking videos I watch are of celebrity chefs who make dishes and meals the way I like it, with normal ingredients. Specifically, I watch this guy for his meats, this woman for her comfort foods, and this girl for her stir-fry. On most nights I start with the meats guy. He's the same age as me and I'm curious as to how someone my age becomes a celebrity at our age. After I'm done with the meats, I move on to the comfort foods woman. She's single like me and I'm curious as to how someone single becomes a celebrity by marrying and divorcing the right person. I save the stir-fry girl for last. She has a British accent just like the meats guy and the comfort foods woman but I can never get over Chinese people speaking British English like they are from another planet. Speaking of which, the stir-fry girl's from where I'm from originally and I'm curious as to how someone from where I'm from originally becomes a celebrity in anything at all.

A Dentist's Wife

Twice I could have been a dentist's wife but I didn't. The first one, he was in dental school when I was in high school, and his ma said to my ma in front of me something about me and him in ten years and waited for me to smile but I didn't. His ma thought my ma and I'd be impressed with him being in dental school but we weren't. Years later when he became a dentist, including mine, I thought I'd either get free or special treatments from him but I didn't. He did, though, set me up as a guinea pig with his foreign dentist friend who fixed my cavity for free to pass his Canadian licence exam in Halifax, and this one, he thought I'd jump at the chance to marry a dentist, but I didn't. He told this to a group of women who'd have gladly married themselves or their daughters off to a dentist and one of them who knew us told my ma who told me to think about being a dentist's wife and having a good life, but I didn't. Back then I wanted to marry someone who couldn't afford to go to a dentist, but he didn't.

Alice Chats Sky

Alice from the office knows I'm Taiwanese like her. Her desk's to my left, my seat's to her right. Our coats are left and right of each other in the middle. Alice's accent makes no apologies. Her gaze says I know you are like me, her ponytail sticking out in spades behind her thirty-something head. It's too late to say me no Mandarin so Alice wouldn't chat with me in Mandarin about home stuff, personal stuff, all kinds of stuff under the sky—so she wouldn't chat sky with me around they no Mandarin. In the lunch room, our lunch bags sit right and left. Alice's homemade bento has a bed of rice, my homemade bento has a bigger bed of rice. We are no blood sisters but our blood is the same shade of carbohydrates and monosodium glutamate. I usually stuff myself while Alice chats sky about the usual stuff, her cellphone to her left, my cellphone to my right.

Q

Once or twice a week the sky cracks an egg over the neighborhood. Moms in the park fuss over the white stuff and wipe it all over themselves and the kids. Dogs I've never seen before are out with dog owners I've not pinged before. This Chinese man who always dresses like he's in the North Pole drags his moon boots in waltz time. When it's time to eat, I break the yolk and tell hubby breakfast for dinner's served. He's over easy at 6'2" and by 6:30 my sexy oven's baked to a ramen Q. That's what you say in Taiwan when the food's chewy. QQ for double chewy. Is it just me or do you see two eggs swimming with short-legged sperms? Is that why some of them don't make it?

Middle America

That time I cried on the tarmac of LAX I thought the flight attendant was going to make me blow into a paper bag. She was a nice and pretty lady and I had an aisle seat. She thought I was afraid of flying and brought me water. Always it was the second leg of the fourteen-hour trip over the Pacific, when you knew you were back on North American soil, that made me feel like the world was not round. It was its own shadow chasing itself in circles. Always here, not there. Always there, not here. I looked into the flight attendant's perfectly made-up face knowing she must have seen it all. Ah, I see, she said, it's someone. Then as if deciding there was nothing more she could do, she gave me a squeeze on the shoulder and moved away to let the other passengers through. A fat man sat down next to me before takeoff, filling his seat and a portion of mine like Valium. I woke up later somewhere over Middle America. A mother with a colicky baby was pacing back and forth by the emergency exit.

Riots

It's one of those things you are here to see, the arc. It's right there. You are here. A block ahead, men and women stand in yellow vests, the kind with reflective silver strips. They are what's standing between you and the arc, the vests. You walk up slowly. Shouts in the language of love are hurled at the arc, at the police standing between the vests and the arc. You walk closer to see the avenue you are here to walk on. Tear gas is fired. There's smoke. The arc's smoking. You detour, retrace your steps from before lunch, a croque monsieur à la fine dining on a sidewalk. You keep walking, away from the vests now gathering in herds, until a petite older woman comes up to you speaking in the language of love you don't understand. You ask for the river and follow her finger. Then, by the river, police in black bulletproof vests are patrolling with big guns and photobombing shots of the city. Soon it's dark. You walk back to your room. The same prostitute from the night before stands in the same corner, outside where you order café crème and croissant in the morning. It bothers you you're both yellow and even though neither one of you wears a vest, she reapplies her rouge when she sees you coming and sees you stealing glances at her and smiles like you know why.

V

My Father-in-Law

My father-in-law was an ear, nose, and throat doctor who liked his steak and potatoes. He died of natural causes in his sleep the year before I met my husband, so I was one year too late in meeting my father-in-law who drove a Jeep and liked his steak and potatoes. And beers, my husband says. What about Chinese food? I ask. Did I tell you, we used to have Chinese takeout once a week and he'd cook his own steak and potatoes? my husband says. I didn't know you had Chinese takeout once a week, I say. He'd eat steak and potatoes for breakfast, too, my husband says. His father was late for breakfast one day. That was how my mother-in-law found him in his room one morning. She got Alzheimer's after that. By the time I met her it was too late to call her Mum, a word that bypasses her when my husband visits and she lights up at the sight of the spitting image of her husband. Your dad looked just like you? I ask. I guess I look just like him, my husband says. What was he like? I ask. Did I tell you, when we were kids, he ran over the cat? my husband says. I didn't know you had a cat, I say. My husband looks up from his laptop and says, We did, and I saw my father pick it up and put it in the trash can.

From Hollywood

I watched a movie star from Hollywood pick her nose with her thumb. The craft show was pretty dead before she came into our booth. She was kneeling down to check out the bowls on the bottom shelf and that was when her hand went up and the thumb went in for a hook. She was wearing a pair of those face-covering sunglasses but her dimples gave her away. I kept waiting for her to look over so I could make eye contact with her sunglasses and say something about our pottery, how Ba and Ma made them by hand in our home studio. While I was waiting, I kept going back and forth between saying hello and hi when she looked over. Then she got up and left. I missed what she did with the booger, if she got it. Then I told Ba that a movie star from Hollywood was just in our booth. He was taking a break in the back with his oolong and asked who's that and did she buy anything.

Fried Chicken

Everyone's sitting down to eat, Fred at the head of the table near the bottles, his shirt untucked, his face already red from the wine, his wife, Kim, next to him, scarf around her neck looped twice like a serpent, their son, Jerry, seventeen, leering at the KFC bucket like he wants to fuck it, their baby, Jenny, her hair an accident, picking up her chopsticks and eyeing the drumstick, Fred picking up the drumstick with his chopsticks and putting it in Jenny's bowl of rice, Fred finding the second drumstick and putting it in Jerry's bowl of rice, Kim intercepting a wing with her chopsticks and putting it in Fred's bowl of rice, Fred settling on a thigh and putting the wing from Kim in Kim's bowl of rice, Kim telling Jenny to eat the breast, Kim telling Jerry to eat the rest, Jerry thinking about thighs, Jenny thinking about legs, Kim thinking about wings, Fred thinking about skins.

Insect Killers

Jenny has a small room. Jerry has a bigger small room. Kim and Fred have the biggest small room. There's one hallway where the four of them avoid each other on the way to their rooms or the bathroom. They pack and unpack themselves in that bathroom. It's long and narrow. The mirror's as long and narrow as the strait they used to live by in a different life. They can all fit in the bathroom mirror in a lineup. Fred doesn't like what he sees. Kim sees what she likes. Jerry and Jenny take turns standing on the bathtub wearing shoes and posing as they like. Nobody wears shoes in the house otherwise. They wear drag shoes. Jenny's are a pair of fluffy pink bunnies she drags in and out of her room. Jerry doesn't wear his the day he sneaks home a black kitten and hides it under his pillow. Kim's dragging hers around when she finds the kitten in Jerry's laundry basket and tells Fred there's a rat in the house. Fred puts down mousetraps with cheese and goes to bed thinking of the cockroaches he killed in their old apartment near the strait. He misses his old drag shoes, which doubled as insect killers. Leather top, rubber soles.

Marching Band

Here they go with Fred driving the stick shift home, Kim driving the family van home, Jerry driving the wedding coupe to his honeymoon home, and Jenny driving a rental away from home via the Chi-Cheemaun Ferry. Kim in the van's following behind Fred in the stick. The stick's swerving and spinning across all lanes and back and Kim's thinking there goes the husband to the stick, goes the son to wedlock, goes the daughter to the Chi-Cheemaun. Kim's saying this to Jenny on the phone, the way she typically is with her doomsday voice. Jenny in the rental on the ferry's picturing the airbag exploding in Fred's face. She's thinking that's that, party's over, turn around and, what, go home? Where's Jerry? Where's Jerry every time? Fucking weddings. Finally Kim's saying thank God it's just the stick but Jenny's unsure what God's going to do with a thing like a stick. The ferry's docking and wheels are coming out of the vessel's belly like a marching band. Jenny's starting up the rental. Jenny's idling. Jenny's rolling. Jenny's roaring.

The Blind Spot

Before the construction crew appeared in the middle of the road with those orange traffic cones, she had been sticking to one lane below speed limit and going straight like her husband said. Dvorak was playing on FM. First time driving by herself in the dark in the snow paying attention to road signs in English, she knew something like this would happen, that she'd have to change lanes. She knew all about the blind spot although it was still a myth to her. Back home no one said anything about it and everybody drove no problem on roads smaller than this with more cars than this. She turned off Dvorak and began slowing down. She was getting closer and closer to crashing into the construction crew if she didn't change lanes, and it wasn't until her headlights lit up their faces that she closed one eye and changed lanes right before taking out an orange cone. The truck from behind blasted a long *fff* that both shook and stimulated her. So much so that as she bypassed the crew unscathed and saw one of them making a hand gesture at her that she'd not seen before but had understood by its shape that it was hostile, she mimicked it, tentatively but surely, by lifting her middle finger to the windshield. Then, turning the radio back on, she was pleased to find that Dvorak was still playing.

The Punch

I shot the puck but it hit the goalie. That was Tuesday. The next day the moron looked like this pug-faced avatar I killed fifty-seven times in a video game. That was spring break, senior year. That week everybody I knew went upstate and I went downstairs. Ma pegged socks and underwear on a clothesline tied to a water pipe that gurgled every time Ba flushed the toilet upstairs in the bathroom next to the guest room that was once Bro's. Bro was the best goalie on the block when we were kids. He wore his mask like a pro, sure as hell never took it off in front of the net, and beat up anyone who tripped me. Billy, now a sales associate at Toyota. Jackson, dumb enough to knock up a girl from NorCal and follow her to Canada. Liam, in prison for something no one seemed to know much about. Bro didn't like these guys but he liked them enough to buy a used Corolla from Billy, drive to Toronto for Jackson's shotgun, visit Liam's parents whenever he was home. Like Christmas and Lunar New Year. I used to think I should stop by too, see about getting some info on Sally, Liam's sister. We hung out a few times. Popcorn, movies, parking lots. The last time, in the backseat of her parents' Oldsmobile, she swirled her tongue in my mouth and said I was not bad for a dork. Later, around the time I joined the men's league, I realized girls called you a dork when they liked you but wished you weren't actually so dorky. Sally was the smart one. She got into Yale and never texted. Not even emojis. I was just some dork who made her horny once and I was fine with that. I went out for a beer on Friday. The goalie from Tuesday was there with his broken nose and a knuckled fist. It came out of nowhere and fast, and I saw stars, real ones. I think I even tasted Sally's bubble gum too. Leathery, a hint of strawberry, very masticated.

Asian Man Through the Ages

Asian Man, 25, throws out the guy at second the same way he chucks the phone book down and pumps his chest when Asian Woman says yes to bubble tea. On Saturdays, Asian Man, 35, makes a batch of hand rolls the same way he wraps a diaper around the baby while Asian Woman washes her hair. Inspired by truck commercials featuring men with tools, Asian Man, 45, tackles a DIY home renovation project the same way he shakes his legs in his BMW waiting for the light to change. Asian Man, 55, has his lumbar spine adjusted once a week the same way he has an ejaculation inside Asian Woman roughly every seven days. This shouldn't happen anymore, but every once in a while, Asian Man, 65, loses his zen the same way he tells the Jehovah's Witnesses he's a Buddhist. Whenever there's someone else other than Asian Woman to talk to, Asian Man, 75, rehashes the story about being shortchanged three cents at the store the same way he shoos a fly away. Asian Man, 85, makes a scene in a hospital gown the same way he remembers Asian Woman making a scene in a hospital gown. Asked what he wishes for his birthday, Asian Man, 95, bares what's left of his oolong-stained teeth the same way he tries telling everybody to leave him the fuck alone.

The Bitter Truth

There was an old Taiwanese woman who was bitter as a widow, bitter as a mother, bitter as a grandmother. She would have been bitter as a sister, too, but her brother was not in the picture and her bitterness could not be attributed to him. While on her death bed in the hospital, she asked for her only son. He was in Canada and had to be coerced by his wife to fly home. The old woman didn't really love her son as she felt that he never loved her after he turned thirteen. He had turned out to be just like her dead husband, the high forehead among other things. She also had a way of bringing out her dead husband in her son. Both men were ill-tempered and liked to drink when she was around. Even her grandson, her son's son, had turned out to embody this male prototype. She didn't love any one of them and they naturally didn't love her, and she was bitter about that. Still, the old woman was somewhat satisfied with the fact that she had married the first, birthed the second, contributed to the third. None of them would be who they were without her and she wanted to tell her son that before she died. She wanted to have one last dig at him by telling him that his family would suffer the same fate as hers, because of karma, and that his son and future grandson would not love him just as he did not love her. The old woman's son held her hand for the first time in more than half a century. As she stared at the hospital room ceiling, he informed her that his son and his son's wife were a practicing child-free couple. They lived in New York with their dog. The mongrel's name was Happy and he loved everyone including the doorman. After hearing this, the old woman lived to be a bitter person only for another day.

Notes

"Arigatou, Sayonara" refers to the post-occupation influence of Japanese colonial rule in Taiwan from 1895 to 1945.

The term Chinese Taipei in "Tadpoles" is the permitted naming of Taiwan in international sporting events like the Olympics.

The *student head* in "Girl and Her Hair" refers to the hair restrictions imposed on junior high and high school students in Taiwan between 1969 and 2005.

Peter Pan in "Two Big Macs" refers to the 1954 musical.

Für Elise in "Still Life" is a piece of music composed by Ludwig van Beethoven and played by garbage trucks in Taiwan to let residents know to bring out their trash.

The partial quote "bad crab...best quality heart" in "The Common Trap" is from the 1993 American film *The Joy Luck Club*, which was based on the novel of the same title by Amy Tan.

The song in "Titanic" refers to the theme song for the 1997 film *Titanic*, "My Heart Will Go On," performed by Celine Dion.

The celebrity chefs in "Cooking Videos" are inspired by Jamie Oliver, Nigella Lawson and Ching-He Huang.

"Riots" refers to the Yellow Vests Protests in France that took place in Paris in November 2018.

Acknowledgements

My gratitude goes to the editors of the following journals, in which many of the poems in this collection, sometimes in earlier versions, first appeared:

Apple Valley Review: "Family History," "Still Life" and "Two Years Later"
Atticus Review: "Pinky Swear"
The Cabinet of Heed: "The Bitter Truth"
Cease, Cows: "The Punch"
Geist: "Church on Queen"
Gordon Square Review: "Fried Chicken"
Honey Literary: "Q"
The Ilanot Review: "About a Fish" and "Balloon, Typhoon, Afternoon"
Juked: "The Blind Spot" and "Call Come Call Go"
Kissing Dynamite: "I Spy"
Lantern Review: "A Dentist's Wife" and "Cooking Videos"
The Los Angeles Review: "Alice Chats Sky"
The Malahat Review: "Two Big Macs"
matchbook: "Calculate Life"
Menacing Hedge: "The Fat Nun," "Insect Killers" and "Moon and Back"
No Contact: "Asian Man Through the Ages" and "From Hollywood"
The Northern Appeal: "Black Limousine"
On The Seawall: "Baby Cuz," "Kill Price" and "Lemons"
Okay Donkey: "Titanic"
Oyster River Pages: "My Father-in-Law"
Passages North: "Sleep Stuffed"
The Penn Review: "Million Bucks"
Permafrost Magazine: "Bullying"
Pidgeonholes: "Girl and Her Hair"
Quarter After Eight: "Marching Band"
Qwerty Magazine: "The Common Trap" and "Persimmons"
Room: "In a Gutless Room"

Ruminate: The Waking: "Fake Teeth" and "Pork Fluff"
The Shanghai Literary Review: "Boys From McDonald's"
Sonora Review: "Steal Eat"
Spadina Literary Review: "Lipstick"
The /tɛmz/ Review: "Bok Choy Love" and "In Hidsight"
Thimble Literary Review: "Hot Stuff," "Legs and Pits" and "Middle
          America"
Whale Road Review: "Exhibit A"
Yalobusha Review: "Scarred"
Zone 3: "Rabbit Holes" and "Riots"

"Pork Fluff" is anthologized in *Best Microfiction 2022*.

"The Punch" is anthologized in *Best Microfiction 2024*.

Thank You

Thank you to the team at Sundress Publications for believing in my project and for their expert advice and guidance through every step of the process. Thank you to my editor, Rita Mookerjee, and the rest of the editorial team for their patience and brilliance in making these poems shine.

To my parents and brother for more than I can ever say with any poems or stories.

To Bernie for reading the first draft of everything I write and saying you like them because of your love for me.

To Ollie, Frankie, Ruby, Macy, Junior, and DeeDee for being in my life and keeping me company even when I have nothing to say.

About the Author

Tiffany Hsieh was born in Taiwan and moved to Canada at the age of fourteen. She's the author of the micro chapbook *Little Red* (Quarter Press). She lives in Kingston, Ontario.

Other Sundress Poetry Titles

Still My Father's Son
Nora Hikari
$18

The Parachutist
Jose Hernandez Diaz
$16

Florence
Bess Cooley
$16

Spoke the Dark Matter
Michelle Whittaker
$16

DANGEROUS BODIES/ANGER ODES
stevie redwood
$16

Back to Alabama
Valerie A. Smith
$16

Good Son
Kyle Liang
$16

Grief Slut
Evelyn Berry
$16

Slaughterhouse for Old Wives Tales
Hannah V Warren
$16

Nocturne in Joy
Tatiana Johnson-Boria
$16

Age of Forgiveness
Caleb Curtiss
$16

Another Word for Hunger
Heather Bartlett
$16

Where My Umbilical is Buried
Amanda Galvan-Huynh
$16

Little Houses
Athena Nassar
$16

In Stories We Thunder
V. Ruiz
$16

www.ingramcontent.com/pod-product-compliance
Lightning Source LLC
Chambersburg PA
CBHW021509090426
42739CB00007B/537